For Gregor

First US edition 2021

Library of Congress Catalog Card Number pending
ISBN 978-1-5362-1520-5

21 22 23 24 25 26 APS 10 9 8 7 6 5 4 3 2 1

Printed in Humen, Dongguan, China

This book was typeset in Times New Larson and Triplex Serif.
The illustrations were done in mixed media.

Candlewick Press
99 Dover Street
Somerville, Massachusetts 02144

www.candlewick.com

my pet GOLDFISH

Catherine Rayner

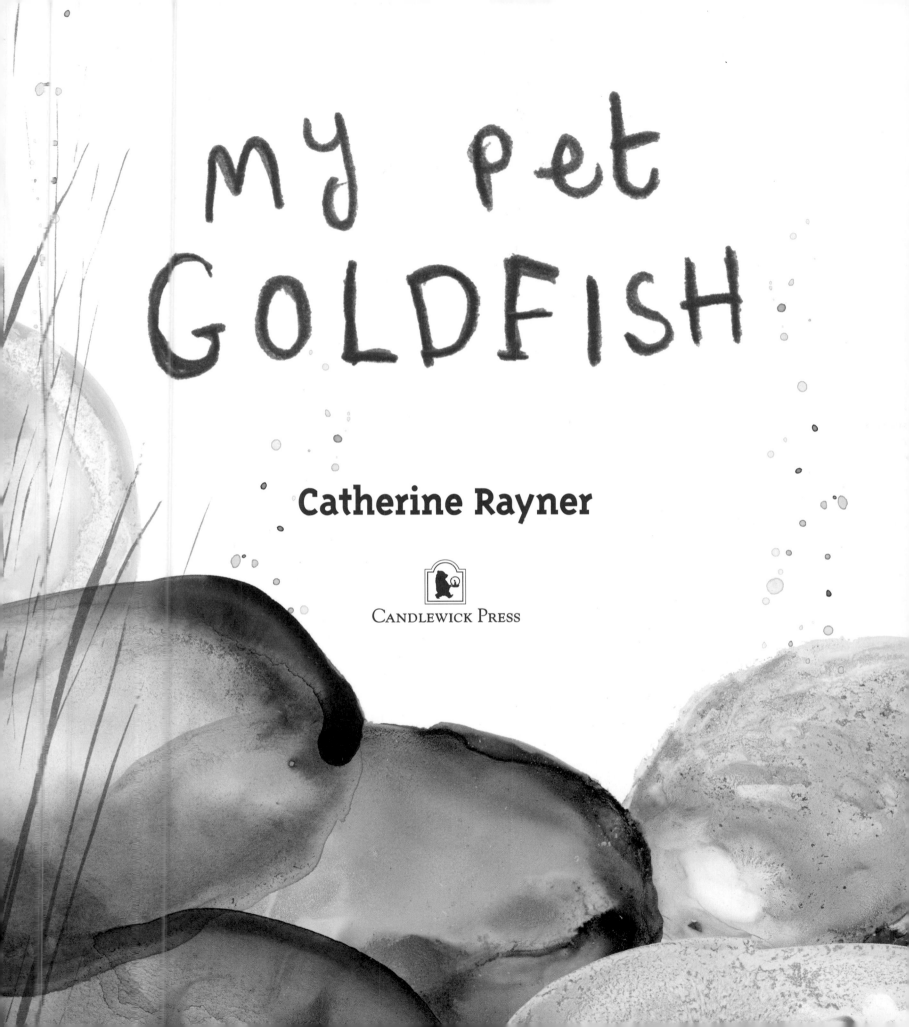

CANDLEWICK PRESS

WHEN I was four, I got my first pet: a fish

no bigger than my hand, with red and orange scales.

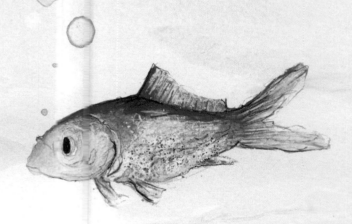

My very own goldfish!

He didn't have a name yet,

so I got to choose one—

and I named him Richard.

Richard came to live in the big tank in our kitchen, with all my sister's fish. There were lots of plants to nibble, rocks to suck, and pebbles to search through for bits of food.

Goldfish have been kept
as pets for more than
a thousand years.

Goldfish need plenty
of space to grow properly, so
you need a BIG tank to keep them in.

5

After school, I would tell Richard about my day. He would swim over when he saw me, wiggling his tail; if I gently touched the glass, he would follow my finger.

People think goldfish forget things quickly, but that can't be right—because Richard definitely knew who I was.

Scientists believe goldfish can remember things for up to five months.

Goldfish have very good eyesight—they can see even more colors than humans.

One day,
my friend Sandy
came over to meet
Richard. Sandy lives
next door and he knows
a LOT about fish.

Richard was hiding—
at first we couldn't see
where. Then we spotted him.

8

"When he's not moving," Sandy told me,

"that means he's taking a nap—even though

his eyes are open. That's because fish don't have eyelids."

Goldfish don't have
lungs like we do—
they breathe using gills.

Goldfish use their eyesight
and sense of smell to find food.

Richard seemed to hear Sandy—he swam up
to the surface and started blowing bubbles.

"He does that when he's hungry," I said, and gave him some fish
flakes. "He likes eating these—but worms are his favorite."
"Worms?" said Sandy. He sounded impressed. "I wonder
if my fish like worms."

A group of goldfish is
called a troubling.

12

Sandy showed me the pond in his backyard—it was full
of goldfish!

They wiggled and whirled through the water, their scales
shining. These fish were MUCH bigger than Richard.

I looked closely. There were some tiny
gray fish, too—the size of dots.

"Look at those ones," I said, pointing.

"Those are the babies," said Sandy. "Their
scales will get brighter as they grow up."

Baby goldfish
are called
fry.

14

Sandy's fish were all different shapes, sizes, and colors—there was even one that looked like it was wearing goggles!

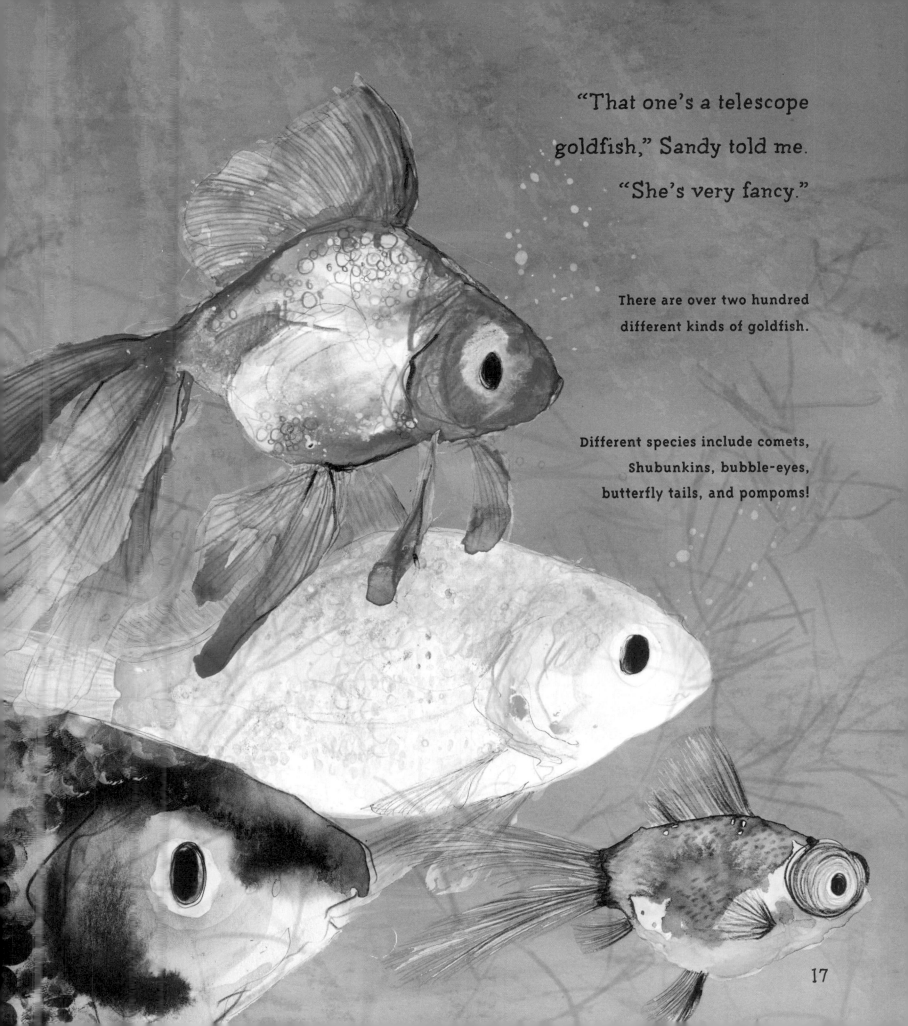

"That one's a telescope goldfish," Sandy told me. "She's very fancy."

There are over two hundred different kinds of goldfish.

Different species include comets, Shubunkins, bubble-eyes, butterfly tails, and pompoms!

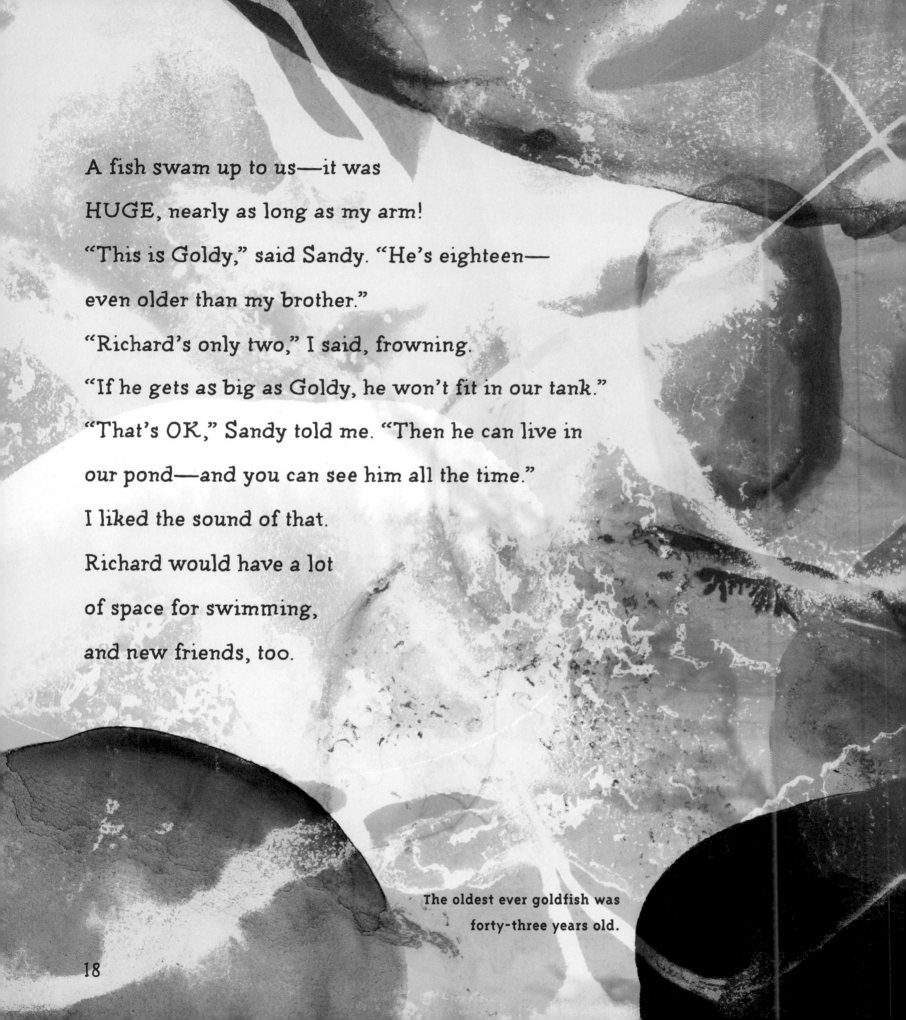

A fish swam up to us—it was
HUGE, nearly as long as my arm!

"This is Goldy," said Sandy. "He's eighteen—
even older than my brother."

"Richard's only two," I said, frowning.
"If he gets as big as Goldy, he won't fit in our tank."

"That's OK," Sandy told me. "Then he can live in
our pond—and you can see him all the time."

I liked the sound of that.
Richard would have a lot
of space for swimming,
and new friends, too.

The oldest ever goldfish was
forty-three years old.

18

Richard grew . . .
  and grew . . .
    and grew . . .

When he was four and a half,
he was finally ready to live in
Sandy's beautiful pond.

Goldfish can grow to be up to 12 inches (30 centimeters) long.

I go and see him all the time. I sit by the edge of the pond and he swims up, doing the same happy little dance and wiggling his tail—as if to say "Remember me?"

23

NOTE FROM THE AUTHOR

The Richard in this story is named after my real goldfish. He's full of character!

I've had goldfish nearly all my life: they make very good pets. If you decide to get a fish of your own, here are a few tips:

YOUR FISH WILL NEED:

o A very large tank to live in, with a filter and an air pump.

o Some good-quality goldfish food.

o   Lots of interesting plants, gravel, and hiding places. (But remember to leave enough space for your fish to swim around happily, especially if you get it some fishy friends!)

o You will need to regularly scoop out about a fifth of the water in the tank and replace it with new water. Before you put the new water in, treat it with special drops from your pet shop. (The drops will keep the chlorine that comes in our tap water from harming your fish.) Also, let the new water sit in a bucket near your tank for at least fifteen minutes before you pour it in so it's the same temperature as the rest—not too hot and not too cold.

o Depending on the climate, goldfish can live happily in a backyard pond, but not any pond will do—please do plenty of research before moving your goldfish outdoors.

INDEX

Look up the pages to find out all about these goldfish things. Remember to look for both kinds of words: **this kind** and **this kind**.

To Find Out More

I very much recommend *How to Look After Your Goldfish* by David Alderton (Leicester, UK: Anness/Armadillo, 2013) as well as the website **thegoldfishtank.com**